THOUGHT
FOR TODAY

THOUGHT FOR TODAY

First Edition 1989

Second Edition January 1990

Third Edition May 1995

ISBN 0-9637396-1-1

Published by the Brahma Kumaris World Spiritual University,
Literature Department, 65 Pound Lane, London NW10 2HH
UK

There are Brahma Kumaris Centres in
over 62 countries worldwide.

Copyright © Brahma Kumaris World Spiritual University
65 Pound Lane, London, NW10 2HH UK

Printed by Waterside Litho, Chesham UK

Available in other languages

*This book has been compiled and edited by the Brahma Kumaris World
Spiritual University, a non-profit organisation, with the aim of sharing
information as a community service for the spiritual growth of individuals.*

C O N T E N T S

PREFACE

The Brahma Kumaris World Spiritual University is dedicated to the moral and spiritual upliftment of humanity. A non-profit organisation affiliated to the Department of Public Information of the United Nations, it is independent of traditional politics or religion. It has had consultative status with the UN Economic and Social Council since 1983 and with UNICEF since 1988.

Established in India in 1937, the University is represented worldwide by 3700 centres in more than 62 countries. The University's primary aim has always been to impart a practical ethical education so that individuals may transform their own lives by tapping the full reservoir of their potential creative energies and channelling those energies in positive directions. Ultimately, this transformation on the individual level will lead to a beneficial change in society as a whole.

INTRODUCTION

Thoughts are food for the mind. A new thought every day will provide the nutrition and stimulus needed to keep the mind healthy and enthusiastic about life. This is becoming increasingly important in the present-day world of disruption and chaos.

Below are the seven main virtues which appear in this book. Each day, choose the one which reflects the way in which you wish to begin the day. Then take a thought at random. Entertain the idea in your mind and see how you and others can benefit from the inspiration you receive. This simple, enjoyable process will focus your thoughts and enable you to develop positivity and strength of character.

Contentment

Peace

Love

Power

Knowledge

Purity

Mercy

CONTENTMENT

Contentment is the happiness beyond the senses.
Living in the moment, I am not lost in the gentle
pulls of the winds, not using the eyes to see that
which lightens and brightens, not using the ears to
be hypnotised by the musicale magnifique and not
using the mouth to taste the sweetness of the first
fruit of the season. I can sit alone with myself,
quietly, silently, with thoughts turned within,
listening to the sound of silence.

Then, I can turn my thoughts beyond the physical,
and tune with the spiritual, the peaceful, the pure.
I have few thoughts. I experience the union with
my spiritual Father, the contented one.

Experiencing His peace, I am peaceful.
Experiencing His love, I am loveful.
Experiencing His contentment, I am content.

Even with a small bank account,
those who are content
find themselves with great wealth.

❊   ❊   ❊

Freedom starts in the mind,
not by cutting ropes.

❊   ❊   ❊

To give happiness to others
is a great act of charity.

❊   ❊   ❊

Cheerfulness keeps up the spirits
of the one who possesses it
and brings a smile to the lips of others.

❊   ❊   ❊

A smile can make short work
of any difficulty.

Happiness is experienced by considering problems to be a game.

❊ ❊ ❊

To taste the sweetness of life, you must have the power to forget the past.

❊ ❊ ❊

Waste thoughts make me heavy and tired; positive thoughts make me happy, light and refreshed.

❊ ❊ ❊

When there is love in my heart, there is life.

❊ ❊ ❊

Balance is the real foundation of a blissful life. With this in mind, my present and future will always remain bright.

Contentment and bliss go hand in hand.

❊   ❊   ❊

*If every step is taken in the remembrance
of God, just imagine how much fortune
there is in every moment.*

❊   ❊   ❊

*If through some error
yesterday was lost in grief,
don't lose today by
keeping it in your memory.*

❊   ❊   ❊

Cheerfulness is the beauty of the face.

❊   ❊   ❊

*Life is like a drama.
If I understand that all individuals
have to play their own parts,
there is great happiness.*

The more I enjoy putting in good efforts,
the greater will be my happiness on
receiving the fruits of those efforts.

❊　　❊　　❊

I must enjoy myself and have recreation,
but I must check whether
it enriches my life.

❊　　❊　　❊

If I make this moment happy,
it will increase my chances
of making the next moment happy also.

❊　　❊　　❊

When I smile, not only do I feel happy,
but also I bring a ray of light
into the lives of others.

❊　　❊　　❊

To have balance in all situations is the key
to happiness.

*In situations of conflict, I have to realise
that the only weapons I need are
a smile and a loveful attitude.*

❄   ❄   ❄

*Sometimes a smile can be like
a drop of water in a desert.*

❄   ❄   ❄

*The wealth of the rich can be stolen or
burnt, but the happiness and wisdom
of the wise remain.*

❄   ❄   ❄

*Opportunities come by creation,
not by chance.*

❄   ❄   ❄

*Individuals are pronounced great
when they can face difficult situations
with happiness.*

Physical beauty can be lost with marks
of age or through accident.
Spiritual beauty can never be destroyed.

❄   ❄   ❄

The person who is honest
and has a true heart
will always feel light and tension-free.

❄   ❄   ❄

True victory means complete control
over the sense organs.

❄   ❄   ❄

If my mind is caught in bondages and
problems of the past,
I will not experience the joys of the present.

❄   ❄   ❄

If I want to advance in life, I must make
sure that my 'wants' don't advance.

To forget troubles, remember God.

❄   ❄   ❄

*If I wanted something and I didn't get it,
maybe I don't need it.*

❄   ❄   ❄

*Condition the mind and remain cool
under all conditions.*

❄   ❄   ❄

*In the long run,
the most difficult thing
is to search for an easy way out.*

❄   ❄   ❄

*When I try my best and this is not
enough, leave it in the hands of God.*

❄   ❄   ❄

*Remember that 'I am very special'.
No one can play my role better than I.*

*Loneliness comes when I forget
that God is my Supreme companion.*

✸   ✸   ✸

*Nothing is just coincidence; every tree in
life's garden bears significance.*

✸   ✸   ✸

*True love is based on understanding
rather than on emotions.*

✸   ✸   ✸

*The one who knows how to adjust
is the one who knows how to survive.*

✸   ✸   ✸

*To age is not a problem, but
by taking on problems, I will age.*

✸   ✸   ✸

*Powerful thoughts create energy in the
mind. Never doubt my ability
to achieve the goal.*

*After a setback, new efforts
bring new growth.*

❉ ❉ ❉

Just being happy helps others along.

❉ ❉ ❉

*When the world becomes like a wild
storm, the most beautiful shelter is God.*

❉ ❉ ❉

*If I do everything with the feeling of
happiness, there will be no task
too difficult to perform.*

❉ ❉ ❉

*The more I understand myself, the easier
it is to remain happy and peaceful.*

❉ ❉ ❉

*When all my attachments are with God,
my achievements are many.*

❉ ❉ ❉

*When I am content, I am broad-minded,
co-operative and easy to approach.*

PEACE

It may seem almost useless to talk about peace when around us we see a continued state of 'peacelessness'. Peacelessness makes it necessary for us to draw upon our own source of peace.

Consider the flowers. They too live in this peaceless environment. They too have to endure the pollution and decay of the world of nature. Yet, wherever they are found, be it by the congested roadside, near the swamps, in the desert amid the thorns, they are eternally beautiful and fragrant. It is not by chance that flowers are given for every occasion, even the most sorrowful. Flowers call forth images of peace and tranquillity. It is their nature.

We are also like flowers. We are the flowers of the garden of God. In this worldwide garden of everyday hustle and bustle, we too are threatened with polluted and degraded circumstances. Being flowers, we are expected to live in our natural state of peace, spreading fragrance all around us.

When we realise that the original nature of our soul is peace, then we can combine with God who is the Ocean of Peace, and so become the embodiment of peace: living, thinking flowers.

What was the future is happening now.
What happens now becomes the past.
So, why worry?

❊   ❊   ❊

What use are peaceful thoughts
if my mind is angry?

❊   ❊   ❊

If I am impatient to experience the
results of my efforts,
it is like trying to eat unripe fruit.

❊   ❊   ❊

Let me be one to make such efforts
that others can be inspired
to follow my example.

❊   ❊   ❊

The one who can adjust with humility
possesses greatness.

People who are crooked
can never really enjoy peace of mind.
Their tricks tie them into knots.

✻   ✻   ✻

Honest individuals are satisfied with
themselves as much as others
are satisfied with them.

✻   ✻   ✻

Sometimes in life I wear so many masks
that it becomes difficult to see my real self.

✻   ✻   ✻

My thoughts, speech and actions
will be full of confidence if I am sincere
in all tasks.

✻   ✻   ✻

The two greatest healers are
God and time.

A life with an aim is a worthy life.

❄   ❄   ❄

Be yourself! Be natural!
It is far easier than pretending to be
someone else.

❄   ❄   ❄

When I am angry,
a great deal of energy is used up and
wasted. Use energy wisely.

❄   ❄   ❄

Silence gives rest to the mind
and this means giving rest to the body.
Sometimes rest is the only medicine
needed.

❄   ❄   ❄

Calmness and tolerance act like
air-conditioning in a room;
they increase a person's efficiency.

Solutions come easily from a calm mind.

❄   ❄   ❄

*If I am unable to wipe out my tendency
to anger, how can I criticise others
for their lack of ability to
control themselves?*

❄   ❄   ❄

*Success springs from coolness of the mind.
It is a cold iron which cuts and bends
hot iron.*

❄   ❄   ❄

*A simple way to remove fear
is to seek knowledge and understanding.*

❄   ❄   ❄

*Let me be a magnet of peace
so that I can attract peaceless souls
and give them peace.*

If someone speaks to me with anger,
let me be one who pours the soothing
waters of love on the fire.

❄   ❄   ❄

If my face is full of worry,
I will cause others to worry.

❄   ❄   ❄

The end of birth is death.
The end of death is birth.

❄   ❄   ❄

If I cannot find peace within myself,
can there be peace in this world?

❄   ❄   ❄

Sceptics can have no peace.
So how can there be happiness for people
who lack peace of mind?

God has a broad back;
if I have a burden,
let God take it from me.

* * *

Silence is absence of sound.
It is stillness
and balance of the mind.

* * *

If I enjoy praise, it means I can easily
be hurt by defamation.

* * *

Only when I accept the rules of freedom
can I call myself free.

* * *

If every morning I can spend a few
moments to sort out my thoughts
and remember God,
the day will be filled with newness.

*When I burn with the fire of anger,
smoke gets in my eyes.*

❊ ❊ ❊

*Where wisdom is called for,
force is of little use.*

❊ ❊ ❊

*When I get angry,
I lose more than my temper.*

❊ ❊ ❊

*No one can make a fool of the person
who keeps cool.*

❊ ❊ ❊

*The harmony that exists within the minds
of individuals will be reflected
in a harmonious society.*

❊ ❊ ❊

*If I allow things to surprise me,
I will get confused.*

*Real temperature control
is to extinguish the heat of anger.*

❀   ❀   ❀

*Weapons by themselves are not
dangerous; it is anger within people
that is harmful.*

❀   ❀   ❀

*If I realised that wars are born in the
mind, I would make greater efforts
for peace of mind.*

❀   ❀   ❀

*If I wish to advocate peace,
do I have to shout and scream?*

❀   ❀   ❀

*The habits of guessing and assumption
can be like ferocious lions.
So do not allow them to run wild.*

When I am looking for solutions,
I must always be ready for surprises.

✤ ✤ ✤

A rose can live amongst the thorns
and yet never be injured by them.

✤ ✤ ✤

If I come to know myself better,
I will gain a better understanding
of other people and situations around me.

✤ ✤ ✤

People with bad tempers are really
angry with themselves.

✤ ✤ ✤

The less I speak,
the more I am listened to.

If I always do my best,
I will be free from regrets.

❄   ❄   ❄

When I change,
the world can change.

❄   ❄   ❄

If I throw a stone into a pond,
the ripples come straight back to me.

❄   ❄   ❄

Let peace be part of you.

LOVE

Love is a powerful force. It can take us to great heights and leave us feeling light and airy. Yet it has been the most abused and misused force. Many degraded things pass for love.

There is a popular song which states: 'What the world needs now is love, sweet love'. What the world actually needs is an accurate and correct understanding of love. True love is based on understanding, mutual trust and respect and not simply on transient emotions.

Love is being in balance, that is, in harmony with the self, God and each other. Love is selfless. Love is not an emotional state confined to whims and fancies, but a transcendent state of consciousness which goes beyond the bodily forms. Love has nothing to do with bodies. Love dwells in the soul. We must allow this love to flow out and around us. By allowing our love to flow, we become moistened and remain forever fresh, attractive and healthy.

Without love, all of life's treasures are locked away from our vision and experiences, for indeed 'love is the key'.

Carry out self-service and the service of others with love.

❄   ❄   ❄

Every situation in life must be faced, and so why not face it with love?

❄   ❄   ❄

If I always wear the costume of humility, I will receive the love and co-operation of others.

❄   ❄   ❄

Being patient helps me to understand why things are taking some time.

❄   ❄   ❄

Happiness is lost when any thought of envy or hatred creeps in. Thoughts of love and good wishes cure sorrow.

The only way to gain respect is firstly to give it.

❊ ❊ ❊

No one tortures me except my impure nature. If I make my nature sweet and lovable, I will win the love of all.

❊ ❊ ❊

Let me be just as enthusiastic about the success of others as I am about my own success.

❊ ❊ ❊

It does not cost a cent to speak loveful, true, sweet words.

❊ ❊ ❊

If I am loving, sweet and co-operative in company, I am valuable.

*One word spoken with love
can soothe a sorrowful heart.*

❊ ❊ ❊

*Rather than being selective,
give regard to all.*

❊ ❊ ❊

*Jealousy cannot exist if I know
my real quality is to love.*

❊ ❊ ❊

*God makes us fragrant flowers.
Am I speaking sweetly to all?*

❊ ❊ ❊

*Without simplicity, I cannot gain
the true affection of others.*

❊ ❊ ❊

*I am a great believer in luck.
The harder I work, the more of it I have.*

*The giving of love and mercy to others
is also a form of charity.*

❄   ❄   ❄

*Having respect for the self and love
for God makes it easy to appreciate
other people.*

❄   ❄   ❄

*No matter how bad people may seem,
they possess at least one virtue.
Be like the humming bird and pick out
the sweetness of everyone's character.*

❄   ❄   ❄

*Is it possible to have unity in a nation
when individuals feel that they are better
than their neighbours?*

*Everybody is attracted by beauty
and qualifications. It is a rare quality to
help the ugly and unqualified.*

*If a task is performed with love,
there is instant success.*

*The more love I give, the more I receive;
the more I have, the easier it becomes
to give.*

*The beauty of all things lies in my ability
to appreciate them.*

*If I avoid others because of their skin
colour, it is the same as hating people
because of the clothes they wear.*

Everyone needs company.
Do I have enough love to share my
company with someone?

❄   ❄   ❄

If I love someone,
I try to be like that person.
If I love God, I will attempt to be godly.

❄   ❄   ❄

Love is universal. It has no limits.

❄   ❄   ❄

Love that hurts is not love at all.

❄   ❄   ❄

When promises are not kept,
close friends are lost.

❄   ❄   ❄

Have equal love for all and experience
a life of equanimity.

When one will not, two cannot quarrel.

❄   ❄   ❄

I am shaped and fashioned
by what I love.
See what happens when I love God!

❄   ❄   ❄

The more I help others,
the more I am kind to myself.
Help others daily!

❄   ❄   ❄

To have love for God is to love humanity.

❄   ❄   ❄

Sometimes I put out a helping hand to
people and they reject it.
In such situations, let me continue
to have loving and merciful thoughts.

A generous heart will quickly become
a precious heart.

❄   ❄   ❄

The best way to conquer enemies
is to make them friends.

❄   ❄   ❄

Learning to know and accept myself
frees me from hatred of others.

❄   ❄   ❄

I am who I am.
So, let me enjoy being this.

❄   ❄   ❄

If I see everyone as family,
it becomes easy to remain loveful.

❄   ❄   ❄

Do not expect love and attention.
Give it instead.

Tears of love do not cause sorrow.
They become pearls.

✳   ✳   ✳

Love has nothing to do with bodies.
Love dwells in the soul.

✳   ✳   ✳

In a bitter world, one drop of true love
is an ocean in the desert.

✳   ✳   ✳

Love is a great power.
It takes great power to have pure love.

✳   ✳   ✳

A task performed with love
needs no thanks.
It brings its own reward.

Sometimes love is allowing someone
to make a mistake so that
they can learn the lesson quickly.

❋   ❋   ❋

To perform daily tasks with a clean
and joyful mind
is love in action.

❋   ❋   ❋

Have as much power as love!

POWER

Power is determination to reach the goal, even
though sometimes that goal seems distant and
unattainable. Gaze at the waves! The caps of white
rise tall like snow-capped mountains. They surge
and move forward, with crowns; crowns of purity
and power, majestic masters.

I observe the motion of the waves. That motion is
relentless. The waves are unaffected by objects in
their path, whether dull or glittering, large or small.
They are tireless, not knowing the word 'obstacles'.

Power is being confident that, though a few battles
may be lost, the great war will be won. It is being a
conqueror. Nothing attracts or distracts. I am
strong-willed. I am fearless. I have no weak
thoughts of doubt. I find impurities within and
have the strength to destroy them, as a brave
warrior. I am stable in the awareness that I am a
child of God, the almighty authority, and being an
obedient child, I have the right to claim that
authority.

*Many people use anger as a weapon.
When I keep humility as my armour,
there is protection.*

❄   ❄   ❄

*If I realise that all people are individuals
with their unique parts to play, the power
of tolerance is easy to develop.*

❄   ❄   ❄

*When there is the feeling that I have to
tolerate a great deal, it means
that I am not tolerating at all.*

❄   ❄   ❄

*If I allow myself to be dependent on
praise and fame, insult and defamation
will destroy me.*

❄   ❄   ❄

*There are two things - action and the
impact of the action. Even if the action is
ordinary, the impact must be positive,
productive and creative.*

When there is faith and victory in the mind, success can be gained. If the thoughts are weak, there will be defeat.

❉   ❉   ❉

Do not allow anything to be an obstacle. See everything as a stepping stone to victory.

❉   ❉   ❉

My controlling power should be such that I have only thoughts that are desired. I create no more than I need.

❉   ❉   ❉

Apply a full stop to unproductive thoughts, feelings and actions of yesterday so that not a trace of them remains.

❉   ❉   ❉

Fear is simply faith in the dark forces. Stay in the light!

A loveful command does not arouse
hostility. It makes the person great.

❊   ❊   ❊

All friendly feelings towards others come
from the friendly feelings I have for myself.

❊   ❊   ❊

If I have to use a stern eye, all right,
but never use hands to create violence.
It shows weakness.

❊   ❊   ❊

Having fear means that I am a danger
to myself as well as to others.

❊   ❊   ❊

Past is past.

❊   ❊   ❊

A powerful person makes others powerful.

Problems in the world will increase; therefore, increase the capacity for dealing with problems.

※　　　※　　　※

When people cannot stand me because they do not understand me, God will stand by me.

※　　　※　　　※

What I experience now is a result of the past; what I experience in the future depends on what I do now.

※　　　※　　　※

Thoughts are like boomerangs. They keep coming back.

※　　　※　　　※

When there is growth, changes are automatic. If I fear change, how can there be growth?

Unless I develop self-respect, I will remain under someone else's power.

❄   ❄   ❄

If I consider all my actions are for God, every task becomes a pleasure to perform.

❄   ❄   ❄

Optimism converts problems into opportunities.

❄   ❄   ❄

If a task is performed in the consciousness that God is my companion, the impossible becomes possible.

❄   ❄   ❄

It is the hour of trial that makes me great and not the hour of triumph.

❄   ❄   ❄

Thoughts create the atmosphere.

Real power and authority are not power
and authority over others,
but over the self.

※　　※　　※

If I have the habit of minding other
people's business, my business will
become bankrupt.

※　　※　　※

Some people never mature because of
fear of ageing and some because they
refuse to accept responsibility.

※　　※　　※

An honest person never fears
the eyes of a stranger.

※　　※　　※

Take one step with courage and
God will give thousandfold help.

People who truly understand themselves
are able to stand by themselves.

✼ ✼ ✼

Gentleness, love, humility, forgiveness are
the greatest powers in the world.

✼ ✼ ✼

When my associates change their minds,
let me check I don't change my mood.

✼ ✼ ✼

The best way to behave when crisis strikes
is to be brave.

✼ ✼ ✼

I help others with good wishes
and good faith.

✼ ✼ ✼

Faith in God means no fear.

Anyone can learn to be a good speaker,
but how many live in a manner
that others can learn from?

❀   ❀   ❀

The weak and idle mind
cannot create powerful thoughts.

❀   ❀   ❀

To be really independent means
not even to lean on excuses.

❀   ❀   ❀

Self-control will give me unlimited control.

❀   ❀   ❀

There is always a chance to change,
but do I make the time to change?

❀   ❀   ❀

When an obstacle comes in my way,
let me stop crying and start trying.

To smile in the face of disaster is the
strength of a stable mind.

❀   ❀   ❀

If people make a fool of me, let me
remember that there is great wisdom
in humility and silence.

❀   ❀   ❀

Accuracy is the strength to retain depth
and stillness inside so that I approach
each second with respect, slowly,
in the right way.

❀   ❀   ❀

Never lose hope. Hope is a rope
on which I swing through life.

❀   ❀   ❀

Some people think a lot and speak a lot
but back down at the time of doing.

❀   ❀   ❀

Self-control is the ability to withdraw and
still the mind at any time.

KNOWLEDGE

Knowledge is essential in order to make a living in this world. However, in order to make living a success, in order to experience every moment of life as new, every day as a day of upliftment and blessing, and to have lasting peace, firstly knowledge of self is of the utmost importance.

'Know thyself', we are told, and so we have travelled far and wide to search for our roots. But we, the children of this world, are orphans.

We have forgotten our Father and we have forgotten ourselves. Knowledge of the self as an immortal, spiritual being is truth. To delve into spiritual matters and experience the self and God is indeed the highest education. God is the Ocean of Knowledge. Knowing God, you can come to know everything.

*If I have the habit of waiting for others,
I will get left behind.*

❄   ❄   ❄

*If I spend an hour in worthwhile action,
there is thousandfold gain. If I waste an
hour in useless action there is thousandfold loss.*

❄   ❄   ❄

*Mistakes are caused by lack of attention;
then there is tension.*

❄   ❄   ❄

*Why try to prove myself? Let others learn
sense through my example.*

❄   ❄   ❄

*Have total faith that whatever is
happening is good, and remain carefree.*

*Before performing any task,
stop for a moment, think of the effect it will
have and then begin.*

❊ ❊ ❊

*It is good to earn money for our needs.
It is the hunger for wealth that
is destructive.*

❊ ❊ ❊

*There are always solutions.
Try approaching the problem from a
different perspective.*

❊ ❊ ❊

*If I am always comparing myself with
other people, I will suffer from either
ego or jealousy.*

❊ ❊ ❊

*It takes self-respect to know how to
remain silent.*

Don't be puzzled by problems, whatever they may be. Always face them as if they are tests to pass.

The four things that have spoiled life are 'I' and 'mine', 'you' and 'yours'. Forget them!

In conflict, if all parties are willing to discuss their needs, there need not be a loser.

The one that forgives gains victory.

No matter how great my words may be, I will be judged by my actions.

To fear death means that I do not
understand the importance of life.

✤   ✤   ✤

Let me not just be concerned about
'rights', but let me consider
whether or not I am right.

✤   ✤   ✤

By acquiring much worldly knowledge,
I could develop arrogance;
with spiritual study there is greater and
greater humility.

✤   ✤   ✤

No matter how hard I worry about a
problem, will my worried mind reach a
solution?

✤   ✤   ✤

Time is life. Wasting time is wasting life.

Self-respect is the foundation of all attainment; its foundation is love.

❄   ❄   ❄

*Treat each mistake as a gift.
I have learned something.
Now move forward.*

❄   ❄   ❄

*If I am dependent on anything,
what will happen when that thing
is no longer available?*

❄   ❄   ❄

*We explore the stars and the depths
of the sea, but how much do we know
about ourselves and the reason
for being here?*

❄   ❄   ❄

*Sometimes I force others to change because
I want them to be how I want them to be.*

*To understand something
I need knowledge, but to feel it
I need experience.*

❅ ❅ ❅

*Have the consciousness of looking after
possessions in trust.*

❅ ❅ ❅

*There is a time to say what I feel
and a time to remain silent.*

❅ ❅ ❅

*The quality of thoughts determines our
degree of happiness.*

❅ ❅ ❅

*If I cling to the past, the present becomes
difficult and the future seems impossible.*

❅ ❅ ❅

Be an actor and not a reactor.

*If there is turmoil internally,
everything outside seems confused.*

❀　　❀　　❀

*Of all the words that I speak,
how many are towards God?*

❀　　❀　　❀

*If I cannot appreciate what I have
at the moment, how can I value what
the future has in store?*

❀　　❀　　❀

*What is more important,
my standard of living or living a life
with ethical standards?*

❀　　❀　　❀

Happiness is the greatest medicine.

❀　　❀　　❀

*Character is not visible in a mirror.
Each expression will leave an impression.*

If angry people feel listened to,
their anger diminishes.

✻　　✻　　✻

There cannot be final results
until I finish the effort.

✻　　✻　　✻

Knowledge combined with understanding
is a simple way to remove fear.

✻　　✻　　✻

Peace of mind comes not from wanting to
change others, but by simply accepting
them as they are.

✻　　✻　　✻

The soul is a jewel in the forehead.
It spreads light to the world.

✻　　✻　　✻

Only after I wake
do I realise I was sleeping.

I must face problems.
It is how I face them that counts.

❄   ❄   ❄

Thoughts become words. Words become
actions. Actions become habits.
Habits become character.
Character becomes destiny.

❄   ❄   ❄

At present, how can I see the future
if I live in the past?

❄   ❄   ❄

Each step in life takes me to
the destination.

❄   ❄   ❄

Whoever has courage can give courage to
others, just as the flame of the candle
can light another's path.

The partner of freedom is always responsibility.

PURITY

Once we were all peaceful and pure, but now our world is one of duality and impurity.

Life's energy has been transformed from pure to impure, from light to dark. The five main pillars of human existence are challenged by their impure counterparts: peace and anger; love and lust; benevolence and greed; independence and attachment; self-respect and false ego.

Purity is so precious, so rare, so powerful that we have to die alive for it. We have to destroy the impure self, the character weakness. We have to love purity so much that it can set us free. Purity is such a mighty force that it can extinguish fires of passion, anger and vice. In their place glows pure, cool love.

Purity earns us the right to come close to God.

As thoughts are the seeds of all actions,
let me plant only good, pure seeds
so that the fruit will be the best.

❄ ❄ ❄

Relationships based on falsehood
are like houses built with their foundations
in mud.

❄ ❄ ❄

If I always hide from the truth, I must be
enjoying the company of falsehood.

❄ ❄ ❄

See the specialities of everyone.
Why focus on another's weakness?

❄ ❄ ❄

Eyes are windows to the soul through
which both our purities and impurities
are revealed.

If I am honest in all my dealings,
I can never experience fear.

✻ ✻ ✻

Let go of thoughts that are damaging
to others and make life
as valuable as a diamond.

✻ ✻ ✻

When there is no love, there cannot be
peace. When there is no purity,
there cannot be love.

✻ ✻ ✻

When I smile, not only do I feel happy,
but I also bring a ray of hope into the
lives of others.

✻ ✻ ✻

If truth and honesty come easily to me,
love from God also comes easily.

*Very fortunate are people who have
learned to admire but not to envy.*

❄   ❄   ❄

Pure is simple.

❄   ❄   ❄

*Let my eyes be a mirror for others,
reflecting only the best and finest qualities.*

❄   ❄   ❄

*Nearness to God is sustained by the twin
virtues of gentleness and humility.*

❄   ❄   ❄

*False humility and ego are the extremes;
in the centre is self-respect.*

❄   ❄   ❄

*If my intentions are pure,
things will eventually work out.*

❄   ❄   ❄

Pure words are powerful healers.

*If a society loses its moral values,
it loses everything.*

✿ ✿ ✿

*Good, clean competition is healthy, but
competitiveness is a fatal illness.*

✿ ✿ ✿

*God is the Ocean of Virtues.
If I am burning with any vice, let me take
a dip in the Ocean!*

✿ ✿ ✿

*It is better to give a handful of rice
with love and honesty than to give
a thousand dollars with the desire for
name and fame.*

✿ ✿ ✿

*Pure thoughts and words uplift
the atmosphere.*

If I put a hood over my eyes,
I will not see anything. The worst hood
is falsehood.

❊   ❊   ❊

Do my thoughts qualify me to claim the
title of 'Child of God'?

❊   ❊   ❊

A special talent used for selfish gain
will change into a shackle.

❊   ❊   ❊

Have quiet consideration for others.

❊   ❊   ❊

The lotus is the symbol of purity.
Its roots are in the mud, but the flower
remains above dirty water.
Live a lotus life. Be in the world,
but unaffected by impurities.

The more I look for defects in others,
the more I will become affected.
Weaknesses are contagious.

❄   ❄   ❄

I may forget my virtues, but God
never forgets.

❄   ❄   ❄

Air and water purifiers are used to
combat pollution in the environment.
How about combating pollution
in the mind?

❄   ❄   ❄

Strength of character is the only solution
to the most difficult problems faced
by the world .

❄   ❄   ❄

The lie I tell today will force me to lie
again tomorrow.

The search for self requires honesty
with the self.

✳   ✳   ✳

One should be simple but not stupid.

✳   ✳   ✳

My conscience is a good friend; let me be
determined to listen to it more often.

✳   ✳   ✳

To fulfil God's desires
is to fulfil my desires.

✳   ✳   ✳

To be a child of God means to display
God's qualities.

✳   ✳   ✳

If I do wrong, let me not try to prove I am
right. Let me apologise
and make amends.

*If I do not clear up doubts in my mind,
it is like allowing a cancer to grow.*

❈ ❈ ❈

If the heart is clean, all hopes are fulfilled.

❈ ❈ ❈

*Without adherence to moral and spiritual
values, there can never be true freedom.*

❈ ❈ ❈

*If thoughts are pure, it becomes easy to
say what I think and do what I say.*

❈ ❈ ❈

*If wealth is lost, nothing is lost;
if health is lost, something is lost;
if character is lost, all is lost.*

❈ ❈ ❈

*There is great beauty in simplicity.
That which is simple is close to the truth.*

MERCY

To the world, the murderer condemned to die has no mercy. To the murderer, the world has no mercy. So the long, strong chain of our inhumanity to our family continues. One person judges another and extracts the price to be paid.

To show mercy is not a sign of weakness in character. Rather, it is a sign of great strength, vision and wisdom. To be merciful is to show an accurate understanding of the situations in life which go way beyond the facts and evidence as they are presented visibly.

To be merciful indicates an elevated consciousness, so high that in spite of the disparities and bad actions, we can have the strength to say 'I understand and I forgive'.

*Misunderstanding can be erased
by loveful, pure thoughts and giving
understanding at the appropriate time.*

❄ ❄ ❄

*If others defame or insult me, let me
shower them with smiles and good wishes.*

❄ ❄ ❄

*When others are annoyed with me and
are saying critical things, if I question
why, it is like pouring oil on a fire.*

❄ ❄ ❄

*If I keep the weaknesses of others in my
mind, they soon become a part of me.*

❄ ❄ ❄

*When the mind is tired, every single
action requires great effort.*

In all moods, discipline gently holds you
steady. Discipline is mercy.

❄   ❄   ❄

When others make mistakes,
let me not keep counting those mistakes.
Instead, let my merciful attitude help them
to overcome the mistakes.

❄   ❄   ❄

A slip of the foot I may recover, but a slip
of the tongue leaves a deep imprint.

❄   ❄   ❄

God has love even for sinners.
All are children of God, and so what right
do I have to judge a child of God?

It is more dangerous to weep inside my mind than to weep in the open. The open tears can be easily wiped away, but secret tears create scars.

❖   ❖   ❖

In the world, many people remain hungry because of the greed of others. If we all knew how to share, the problem would be solved.

❖   ❖   ❖

To have the use of the eyes is a very special gift. Let me be one to give love, peace and happiness to others through my eyes.

❖   ❖   ❖

Rather than feel that I am competing against someone, it is better to have the feeling that I am helping everyone.

Why not be instrumental in solving the problems of others instead of being a problem?

❄   ❄   ❄

It is better to make use of a chance to change than to try and change your chances.

❄   ❄   ❄

If clouds remain in the mind, water will fall from the eyes.

❄   ❄   ❄

Which causes the most pain, the mistake or the criticism for the mistake?

❄   ❄   ❄

Even if I am sick and become a patient, I must never lose patience.

If I get involved in fears about the future,
I shall miss the chances that the present
offers me.

❋ ❋ ❋

The monarchs among us are those who
put others first and serve everyone.

❋ ❋ ❋

Loneliness is often the result of a lack
of ability to communicate.

❋ ❋ ❋

I am limited in the amount of help
I can give to others. It is far better
to help a soul come closer to God.
Then all help is received.

*If I misuse my talents and virtues,
I am the only one to lose.*

❆   ❆   ❆

The truth is that truth is.

❆   ❆   ❆

*I may say I know, but by my actions
I am known.*

❆   ❆   ❆

*Pure love is the basis of eternal
relationships.*

❆   ❆   ❆

*Always have good wishes and pure
feelings for others.*

❆   ❆   ❆

*At any moment I could start being a
better person.
Which moment shall I choose?*

To laugh at someone else's misfortune
is to display ignorance.

* * *

Sometimes, owing to jealousy,
I try to degrade others. In so doing,
I degrade myself.

* * *

If I am proud of myself, very quickly
I will reach the stage in which
I despise others.

* * *

If I care only for myself, others will begin
to care less about me.

* * *

The only definite thing about human
beings is that they change.

The greatest service is to share with others
the joys of living.

✻ ✻ ✻

It is one thing to tolerate someone's
mistake. It is something even greater to
forgive the mistake.

✻ ✻ ✻

When I observe the beauty that is within
God, it becomes so easy to appreciate the
beauty within Creation.

✻ ✻ ✻

The account of peace and happiness is
credited when God is remembered.

✻ ✻ ✻

Being co-operative does not mean
becoming a slave.

Do not lose hope in those who
have lost hope.

❄   ❄   ❄

Be firm when authority is required,
but be gentle and sweet when
administering authority.

❄   ❄   ❄

In all respects keep giving respect.

❄   ❄   ❄

One way to guard against feelings of hate
is to give regard.

❄   ❄   ❄

Sometimes the greatest contribution I can
make is to give regard.

❄   ❄   ❄

If someone keeps laughing at me,
I don't need to fret. At least I am giving
happiness.

When I agree with people who gossip,
I will be the next one they slander.

❄ ❄ ❄

To remain cheerful, congratulate the self
and congratulate others on their
specialities.

❄ ❄ ❄

If I blame others to protect myself,
time has a way of revealing truth.

❄ ❄ ❄

My specialities influence others.
So, let me use them well.

❄ ❄ ❄

There is nothing more nourishing
than happiness.

❄ ❄ ❄

Forgiveness is the noblest form of revenge.

To give happiness to others
is a great act of charity.

❄ ❄ ❄

Can someone who causes pain to others
experience real joy?

❄ ❄ ❄

The moment I insult someone is the
moment I lose others' respect.

❄ ❄ ❄

I am my own best friend and worst enemy.
Let me make effort to uplift myself and
not to degrade myself.

❄ ❄ ❄

True forgiveness means not to make the
mistake again.

❄ ❄ ❄

The best way to rectify a mistake is to
begin with an apology.

THE BRAHMA KUMARIS CENTRES
IN THE UNITED KINGDOM AND IRELAND

LONDON
Global Co-operation House, 65 Pound Lane,
London NW10 2HH
Tel: 0181 459 1400

NUNEHAM COURTENAY
Global Retreat Centre, Nuneham Park,
Nuneham Courtenay, Oxon OX44 9PG
Tel: 01865 343 551

EDINBURGH
20 Polwarth Crescent, Edinburgh EH11 1HW
Tel: 0131 229 7220

CARDIFF
15 Morlais Street, Roath Park, Cardiff CF2 5HQ
Tel: 01222 480 557

DUBLIN, IRELAND
36 Lansdowne Road, Ballsbridge, Dublin 4, Ireland
Tel: 01353 603 967

Introductory courses in meditation are offered at each of our centres
throughout the country, free of charge.
For more information and the address of a centre near you, please contact
one of the above centres.